10,000 WORDS

by John Riley

EXOT BOOKS
NEW YORK

exotbooks.com
First Edition
Copyright 2023 John Riley
All Rights Reserved
Typeset in: Academy Engraved LET & Baltica
ISBN: 978-0-9898984-7-8

Editing — R. Nemo Hill
Design & Photography — Julio M. Perea

The author would like to thank the following journals
in which various versions of these poems
have appeared—

Story of 100-Words
The Abyss
Bindweed
Smokelong Quarterly

Read one of these poems and you'll want to read the others. John Riley has created a severe compositional structure, producing 100 poems of 100 words each. This self-imposed restriction fires his spontaneity. A multitude of images, always deep, never just fanciful, spring from his surreal imagination. Nothing is ponderous, nothing forced. An ending often has the feeling of a beginning, a beginning is like an ending. As with Samuel Beckett, words and phrases and sentences are pools— and the complete 100 word poem is the largest pool, inviting us to jump, then swim or tread water, at our whim.

John Marcus Powell, author of *Black Uncle*

A book of one hundred stones: some heavy, some light, some bigger than they seem, some formed by a river while giving the river its form, some leaving a deep impression, some found in the lowest of places, some unwieldy, some glistening, some crystalline though you can't see through them, some striking against each other to create light, some shaped by having once been broken. Some clonk you on the head and some you have been carrying around this whole time. This book also contains one hundred poems. What I wrote about the stones is true also of the poems.

Walter Ancarrow, author of *Etymologies*

What is poetry anyway? Does anyone know? It won't be there, then you sense a stirring in the grass, and suddenly you're up to your neck in it, and before you can grasp it, it's gone. You are bereft. So you fill the emptiness with intense awareness of the world of things you are sure to lose. Riley's poems are founded on such loss. On the current of his sentences I move through inconclusive lives, charged, and instead of purposeful ideas find thought-magic, an open heart. Heavy and light, like water, his poems sing to the thing that never left.

Cally Conan-Davis, Poet

For My Family,
the whole of them,
wherever they are

Contents

1 Which Stone

2 Bone

3 Go Away

4 Confession

5 Centuries

6 Privilege

7 Rivers, No

8 Ice

9 As If It Were A Stone

10 Victory

11 Leaving The Last House

12 More Stones

13 South Pole

14 Diagnosis

15 Wrong Mountains

16 The Die-In

17 Hole In The Sun

18 He^2

19 First Settler

20 I Never Knew

21 How To Die

22 Ashtray

23 Breaking Bread

24 Copernicus

25 Trains

26 Before Light

27 Seasons

28 Baby

29 Wrong Words

30 Consequences

31 Words Outside

32 Eyelids

33 Visitation Day

34 Dragonfly And Crow

35 Borders

36 Stronger

37 Passion

38 Goat Herder

39 Even Small Deaths Demand Songs

40 Wise Men

41 Bedtime

42 Bottle

43 Great Dismal

44 Down Below

45 Dressing

46 Rising

47 A Country Walk With No Ambition

48 Bluebird Sky

49 Like A Math Problem Looking For Its Sky

50 Window

51 History

52 Night Swimming

53 What Is Left Alongside Her

54 All Fog Is Gray

55 The End Of Some THING

56 First Look Back

57 Ghosting

58 The Road Ahead

59 One Night

60 Night Bells

61 Moon Flag

62 Age Old Stones

63 Creation Story

64 Outside The Gate

65 End

66 Lies

67 Light

68 Hands

69 Lambs

70 Green

71 Street

72 Fingertips

73 Blinking

74 Food

75 Blue Petals

76 Away

77 Shearing

78 Apartments

79 Stay

80 Selfish

81 Silver

82 Marsh

83 Temples

84 Magician

85 Rocks

86 Quiet

87 Dweller

88 Walls

89 Mirage

90 Heaven

91 Clandestine

92 I Knew Her

93 Grief Thievery

94 Worms And Horses

95 Note

96 Nothing

97 Banishment

98 Contours

99 The Glow

100 Free Labor

Forward

This is a book of 100 poems, and each of these poems is strictly 100 words. As for the title, well—do the math. The poems are solid as stones, atomically precise in their particularities and peculiarities, boldly detailed, and yet their powerful musculature seems ephemeral, their boundaries poised near the edge of unsparing dissolution. They seem to contain far more than they reveal, which is why, on reading them, one is left staring at one's empty hand, arrested in the motion of grasping. They are both concrete and ungraspable—which, for me, is the persistent enigma of great poetry.

R. Nemo Hill

The right way to live is something
we can only teach the dead.

Fernando Pessoa

I keep my visions to myself.

Stevie Nicks

1

Which Stone

Is it two steps to the left and then a loop with his right foot pressed down carefully on the next stone washed by the rapid stream? Or is it one step to the left to allow his right foot to reach the stone without making a loop? Other alternatives seem just as logical. He is frozen yards away from the creek side. He had been warned to follow instructions. "Tonight, in this stream, the wandering stops," he was told. But now he struggles to remember his next move, here in the rushing water, alone, inexorably fragmented above fragmented stones.

2

Bone

He has no need to pull up and search for those last bits of bone. There's little chance of finding any. Splinters may have tempted a fox, or been flown away in the beak of the crow nesting above the fig bush. Perhaps he should search closer to the well-house. His feet will leave deeper prints in the soft soil there. Why wonder? He has no cause to search for the bones that fell from the scaffold that once stood in the oak's shadows. He can go now to the coast and watch his moments concentrate sunlight on the sea.

3

Go Away

The world is everything when he can't touch it. He is driving, near dusk, through a sky of mountains leaning over meadows. Brooks, incessantly cold, demand his crooked attention. The stream's black stones are washed by falling water murmuring the mountain's message. Fairy slippers bow to hide their violet heads. He closes his ears, keeps his eyes focused ahead until he sees only approaching cars, each with a smile trapped between dull headlights. Cars are ugly beasts, though some, as with all things, are uglier than others, each with a smirk making him feel like a coward for speeding away.

4

Confession

Only sleeplessness can make him imagine he is sitting beneath an artist's sun, by a swift river, while a dove enters on quiet feet—just as it did long before when the boy, waiting patiently for his Master's cuff, caught a glimpse of centuries of schoolboys snaking past the sting of grace's smack and, from this, ciphered a faith that fed on the fruit of curve and wave. No, it is a dream sprung from another false hope, one that pierces like a spear through a desert's brief blooming—when a sky bluer than blue-blood irises disappears behind a ridge.

5

Centuries

A woman with an ancient face comes to him. Her voice puddles in the bowl she holds before her. "Come," she says, "dip your hands into forever. Sink your feet to where worms plow new homes." He lays his head on her amber shoulder. The darkness comes and the trees wander away. When he turns to follow the moon, she gives him a torch and turns him from the forest. He wanders and wanders and still the song she sang sounds in his head. No death in her song, no tortured gathering of murderous crows, no accumulation of brilliant tears.

6

Privilege

There is one secret he holds tight. Every night, sleeping alone in his stone-walled bedroom, he dreams of flying. —No, that isn't correct. He flies in his dreams as a matter of course. He cannot remember a night when he failed to angle through the sky, soaring like a man of privilege, making sharp turns away from borders. With a certainty stronger than he ever feels when awake, he knows that the land below is his and that it is a privilege to fly in his dreams—of all the privileges he has been afforded, the only one he values.

7

Rivers, No

There have been too many poems of rivers, even of twin rivers that run like furrows plowed by the invisible hand that molded mountains into the clouds. Today we will not go to rivers, currents bouncing into whiteness, out of the dark and shallow waters, to where the soft land opens and the streams begin to float toward the giant gulf that will be their end. We will turn downward instead, into the subterranean world, though there are rivers here too, much slower rivers full of torsos bobbing pointlessly, absent-minded smiles on their faces, consumed by the connivance of centuries.

8

Ice

His head turns to cold things, luxurious in their ice. Fish with fins frozen mid-sway, birds with wings etched on white sky—only clouds moving, leaving all else in place. And humans, mouths open, as though pleading to forces they had refused to question, content now with a force invented. Now, with their jaws locked, huge hills of ice to scream at when the time comes to shatter and leave their magnificence only in the memory of frozen bird or once-weary fish content in its immobility—the damned human head is left to stare at all it refused to know.

9

As If It Were A Stone

The sea itself, the old sailor thought, is the translating craft—it's the time it takes to open the sails each morning, to gather new time in billows through the dazzle of new days, birdless dawns—sailing beyond the horizon, solo, through more full sails than are countable. He's no counting man, he's empty of measurement, and it takes him until now to understand, alone, with no hunger, in the lope of pacific waves—to realize that a way home, when home is still possible, requires him to stand at the bow and search for the illusion of a point.

10

Victory

Still dead, he smells dead horses, fresh dung, hears the screams that linger in the fading sunlight, the ones that float with the smell of sweet courage torched, its acrid smell lingering over the emerald surface of the dead lake. In the deeper distance the string of a black river falls from flowering hills. He is unlike the charred and twisted bodies, arms forged into supplication; unlike the horses, still alive, bridled by the crumbling heat. He watches himself emerge from dust, freed finally from love of the arrow, heading into the hillside birches glowing white as next winter's snow.

11

Leaving The Last House

During this time of life, the question has always been: "Do you have any questions?" It is important to listen to the notes in all that is said, and at night he hopes the music is not lying about the cold. The fog of breath, the slight creak of knuckles when he balls and unballs his fists—this is what sustains him. It is time to leave when the notes become words, moral words with peasant hips spoken by women with extended hands. Then he hurries out the back, around the corner, across the rock garden, to the single oak.

12

More Stones

How long has it been since he forgot all those things he should know? But what-he-should-know is not a thing, he says out loud—yet there is no one to listen. As when the teachers took turns telling him all the things he should know, he sits in his chair in the center of the room and thinks only of stones and how they are all shaped differently, everything locked-up inside, all of the stone beneath their stone surface locked inside, and he wonders if the stones ever dream of being free before the river water turns them to dust?

13

South Pole

The girl with a face that says "Antarctica" walks from behind the bush beyond the department store. She holds a white kitten pressed to her neck. Perhaps the kitten is why she is here. She may have been digging worms in the sick light and feeding them to the kitten, mouth to mouth. The man is there paying a debt to society, making unnecessary purchases, lobbing them lightly into dumpsters. It is the time of day when the sky is most likely to be pink and blue, yet today it is a dull yellow, like the patina of a scream.

14

Diagnosis

When the doctor returns with the news, the man re-
members how his wet hair turned to ice the night
he jumped from his bath and ran across the unfur-
rowed field, water dripping from his bald crotch, his
feet pounding the potato dirt. He is thinking, years
later, of the old tobacco farmer, drunk each day
from dark to dawn, of how the tractor tilted when
it crushed his shoulder. He still hears the old man's
scream snapping across the half-plowed field. He
wants to tell the doctor about the man's question.
He wants again to hear the boy whisper: "Alive?"

16

The Die-In

All night they stand in the pasture, lined up as though preparing for a battle-charge. At first light, they begin falling, one by one, in close proximity, bodies often dropping onto the bodies beside them. The line of cows slowly withers. So many die—they can't all be buried before the gas inside their stomachs turns their bodies onto their backs, legs reaching toward the sky. No one knows why the cows begin dying. Tests fail to explain either deaths or odd death behavior. Those of us on burial duty work around the clock until all the remains are gone.

17

Hole In The Sun

He reads that a hole is growing in the sun and tries
to not think of rivers. Yet when he closes his eyes in
hopes of sleep, it is mere seconds before rivers flow.
He watches the eddies lap the small stones. It's nev-
er a rapid river and for this he is grateful—but now
that he knows the sun's plight, it is his duty to think
of its wide wound. He promises himself he will ig-
nore the dark waters when he closes his eyes, that
he will dream instead of a fire digging through the
sun with a drum.

18

He^2

It is while washing his face in the white tin basin, standing on the horizon of his exhaustion, that He sees He^2. Taller, stronger, and much better rested, He^2 gives He a long look, then smirks. "Is this what you've become," He^2 asks? "You should have followed my suit." He starts to protest. He was not offered the same opportunities. He was first, here to make the way. He^2 shows He his palm. "It's too late to argue," He^2 says. "Go rest your sagging bones." He turns his back to the white tin basin. He^2 never speaks to He again.

19

First Settler

Across the river, he builds a cabin too small to house more bodies than one. After treks to the ship to bring up supplies, he closes the door and waits for nights as black and long as his blade is bright and quick. He hopes for deep night, sitting in the dusk, and longs to see it empty and unadorned, but he sees instead a glowing quarry filled with shining jewels and red fire. The wife he will never marry is there, along with the children he will never hold, and the night is full and the dark is gone.

20

I Never Knew

"Tilt your nose back," my uncle says. Blood runs in two streams across my upper lip and down the sides of my mouth. "You're always staring at the ground. That's probably why the punk popped you." His lips are squeezed shut. He's been in two wars and one prison. When he dies his friend Alejandro will kneel by the casket. His tears will fall to the floor. My mother will stare at him—her lips pressed so tightly together they make a single line. Then she'll look at me and say, "Good. He's dead. His life left us all confused."

21

How To Die

"There are several scenarios that could work," the old town father says. "How about this? Say your mother is a witch who casts spells on the pregnant girls in the village, and you travel home to save her from a mob screaming in the town square. On top of that, you are owed money for throwing charts and the royal bastards are trying to beat you out of it. After the old mom is saved you decide to collect your fees. Of course, there's nothing stopping you—until you come upon a strange town trapped in an orbit gone wrong."

22

Ashtray

This story is a lie struggling to tell the truth. By the time he is a boy he perceives the world as a string of disconnected visions, brought together for an unknown purpose. This concerns him because he's not sure his final vision will roll out as he's planned. Perhaps a new story will begin to weave itself at that last moment. He doesn't know if he can plan his last image any more than he planned the first one. The solution, he thinks, might be to tie the threads of his images together with the finality of a catastrophe.

23

Breaking Bread

He peers through the window with dawning eyes,
charmed by the light. This is honorable, he thinks,
gathering in stillnesses to sit like crowns on the
waving tops of wheat across a field. If he were clos-
er, he could see drops of gold shining on the tops of
the stalks. He has been thinking this way for weeks.
Light is noble, rivers have dignity, the tea table with
fragile legs is bending beneath false manners. He
has more answers than questions. What does his
thinking this way mean? He butters his toast, pulls
the shade, satisfied to have no answer.

24

Copernicus

He orders a beer from the motherly waitress and thinks of what it might be like to yell, "Serving-woman, bring me your stoutest ale!" If he had lived centuries before, would he have been a warrior with the grim knowledge buried in his ignorant heart that soon the arrow would be for him? Or would he have been the faith of a city, full of glowing ambitions, working to gather the wherewithal to make them happen? —An intelligent man in heroic orbit when faces were shiny with meat grease, dreaming of musical time and towers, making near-sighted observations of Mars.

25

Trains

Alone, on the porch, watching college students sprint to the top of the hill, then turn toward the park, spring sun sinking, the weather desired, amiable breezes pushing him to think of racing the final train, the train unleashed, speeding through stops, over trestles, signal-men diving, lantern-lights swinging, always concerned, but never enough, that the molten red rails will buckle, the train will take a flyer off a mountain or slam into a station, cars flying over cars, the conductor crushed, aware all along that he is obsolete, left there to envy the students running up the hill for beauty.

26

Before Light

After sleep, she waits in the doorway that no longer stands. The sheet is wound round his feet. He hangs, a star-blue stalactite, just inches above the ground, hoping she'll slip away before morning forms. When light creeps from beneath the earth, her smile pools like mercury across the floor. She rattles her box of worlds. Come, she says. To go where? To eat dirt with a three-tined fork in a land of fire? He slithers away across the floor. After refusal, she leaves. She never lingers. Now he waits for lungs to fill, for eyes to turn to stone.

27

Seasons

It isn't only the heat that keeps her shiny. Not any longer. She's healthier now. She no longer has to walk the fine borders of sleep, filming herself in mirrors, seeking evidence that she is real. She has all the necessary lives down—the ones out there for different times of day, and the one that flits from poplar to oak to pine. No one is invited to join her when she dances. No tree holds her tight. No limbs keep up with time. She refuses to think of winter, when a cold hand will try to cleave her apart.

28

Baby

When the nurse hands him the baby it is wrapped in thick, pale-blue paper and sealed with yellow tape. He cups his hand beneath the back of the baby's head the way the nurses in the delivery ward had taught him and the soft skull shifts in his palm like not quite formed gelatin. As he turns to leave the room the attending nurse nods toward a utility cart and hisses, "Roll it out!" The woman on the bed stares at him. Thick, wet ribbons of black hair cling to her face. The husband stands beside the bed, watching him.

29

Wrong Words

Winter is a seldom beast. The words appear in her head and she whispers them before she can stop herself—watches her breath fog the glass. Such words have no place and she regrets them when they appear. Winters with their ice seldom come this far south. This is what she means, and she wishes the thought could have come in those words. Instead, she thinks winter is a seldom beast and the words frighten her. The baby is asleep and she wonders if that is why the wrong words come. Now the thought of sleep has a peculiar angle.

30

Consequences

They wait a long time for him to die, then turn and go their ways as he goes his. At first, the townspeople pat each other on the back, but soon the gathering grows quiet, pensive. He goes in the other direction. All in all, it is tiresome being dead—his blood drained out with deep cuts in his femoral arteries—but not much different than before. It could have been worse. He could be carrying his head as he trudges up the side of the first range of hills, trail dust barely stirring when he lifts his weary feet.

31

Words Outside

The searcher counts each day while waiting for the next day, for the next path. When light approaches, he tries speaking outside the words he once spoke. He hopes the dark inside him becomes a light outside. He's convinced there's a creature that uses his voice while he sleeps, a creature that wishes to sound human while existing as single-speaker of the night. Mornings, he wanders. And if a swift walker should pause and ask if the day will ever be here, all the counter can say is it's the next one, waiting alone by the next path, over there.

32

Eyelids

When he closes his eyes, he sees blue passion or, more precisely, he thinks of passion when he sees the field of blue. If he asks himself why he thinks it is passion, he is surprised by the answer—because his eyes are closed. Is he limited to seeing emotions when his eyes are closed? The blue is not always the same hue yet he is unable to make a connection between hue and meaning, or hue and causation. He knows little, nothing actually, about hue or reason or cause, and in this, he is no different than anyone else.

33

Visitation Day

The key is lost and the crowd is waiting. You who are not here imagined much more than we will ever live—and now I wait. There is a desk and a window opening to the balcony I will not stand on to speak to the crowd. I linger beside the inner door, thinking of what awaits us beyond the crowd with their waving torches. Our destination is of no consideration. Our time together must be aimless, with no step taken in unison. We will stroll down the streets with little regard for drivers, walk like music wishing for rain.

34

Dragonfly and Crow

We're left by the fire after the boss stands at the flame's waving edge, wearing black suit and immaculate boots, telling us about the dragonfly and the crow which have bedeviled his every moment since the fire's first spark, and how he's found a solution and will soon be free of their cruelty—how he, the boss, will soon pull off their wings and grind them into dust. Then he turns, the boss, and runs into the flames—. We join hands before spreading blankets on scorched grass, opening bottles of cold beer, sharing figs fatter than those in eternity.

35

Borders

We're well-armed guards, each with his weapon slung across his back, held in place with the stretched skin of the last man who thought we could be stopped, or captured and imprisoned in the holes they dug, or wrapped into a hollow tree with thick vines and broken chains. Fools they were— our weapons are the most powerful, our bullets the fastest, our sight unmatched, our nerves cold as the winter ice that we crack with ancient stones to drink our fill on mornings after we've wiped our weapons with fine oil and cooked our latest catch over smokeless fires.

36

Stronger

He slipped downhill and faced the tunnel. The tunnel's mouth grew smaller the longer he stared, but this did not deter him. He could not be deterred. Once he was down the slippery bank there was no path for him to climb back up. He had no understanding, and no wonder, and he no longer yearned for either. He had no hopes for peace or deep quiet or noise or pain or fear. Once he had tended a fire, but that fire had long since perished and he no longer had to disregard inclinations to understand or desires to escape.

37

Passion

He's a fool now, forgets to stay in gulleys, wanders right across fields, his trek continuous since his banishment. Once, he was praised in his town, lifted up above all men. Once, he was expected to create passion—but without using words. Words, the townsfolk had insisted, were crude tools. His material must be space. "See the emptiness between a tree and a tree?" they'd asked. "Make passion from that!" They'd made it clear that nothing was more important than to see his silent passion. When he failed to create it, after years of effort, he slunk into the wild.

38

Goat Herder

The dogs slip the gate, into the small lot where the goats spend their hours recalling days of being satyrs free to play their flutes for demons on the dry hills above the blue sea, up where stakes wait to be driven into rocky hilltops, up where the temple fires are in need of fresh meat to scorch. The goats dream on until the keeper's dogs, ravaged by timelessness, savage them, leaving them torn and bleeding across the grass where the woman, their tender, is dropping to her knees amidst the flesh, raging like a mother refusing to be comforted.

39

Even Small Deaths Demand Songs

Are all savageries softer in the morning? Or is this only true for we who burn memories the way temple keepers burn incense for a traveler whose mind is full of the snows that blocked the mountain pass? In this dark, nothing but stones can guide our way. By low light, we see the traveler lingering inside the killing barn, though we are too far away to see if there are ribbons in her hair, or if it's held back from her forehead with a thin band spotted with tiny glass beads that fail to shine in the stall's shadows.

40

Wise Men

The wise men have been here an hour and we do not know when they will leave. They have not made their intentions clear as to 1) why are they here, 2) how long they will stay. I feel her eyes burning into my back and do not dare turn around. She scolds me daily for being weak, for missing the ingredient that would allow me to stand up and say thanks for coming by, perhaps we can get together later. She's right. My family requires me to have a spine and I've become convinced I will never have one.

41

Bedtime

When he sleeps on the suspension bridge that hangs between the halves of my town, the river below, the one that moves like a tired clock, is brown, or sometimes black, and is all he has for a pillow. He has been told his face looks like a boiled potato ready for mashing, but all he asks is what could make the river stop flowing. What words could be said, what force could appear, that would vanquish the soft myth the river makes, a myth made of the bluebells that listen to the songs he whispers through the steel grate?

42

Bottle

His minutes will be twisted into a bottle, then set afloat on the shadows cast by buildings creeping in and out of his days—left to roll along the streets, a jingle of glass uncracked, stoppered with a piece of bedsheet pulled from a bed that sits deep among thin pines. No one will read such words today and even he has days when he can't bear him, the subject of his minutes. He is on to him, he thinks now, crossing the street, his hands grimy from wooded sleep, his thoughts pursuing themselves, cars speeding by as though invisible.

43

Great Dismal

Herons, egrets, and cranes explode the night. The swamp should welcome a solitary astronomer, one who has found comfort placing nature's darkest corners on pedestals. Now, I've thrown the universe away, watched it angle like a hat on a windy day. In the blind dark, another cascade of screams warns me. Three steps and I'm waist deep in the bog. Mud beneath my feet shifts, begins to suck me into billions of years of deposits. There will be a starkness to being gone. First, a dark sea of space retreats, then planets vanish, stars disappear, then darkness needs no repair.

44

Down Below

If you want me, look down. There I'll be, between floorboards, or swelling bulges beneath the tiles. Watch the bubbles ripple across the floor, hear the boards groan as they let me through. If there is carpet, I'll have free rein to surface and wander through the room, or perhaps I'll wiggle up the stairs, visit you as you bathe. Then I'll watch you sleep as you try to conjure a soft dream from the desert inside. I know you cannot remember when it was easy to reveal your bedtime wings, gliding through all those arches now crumbled to ash.

45

Dressing

. . . heaviness doesn't come from love or not-love but from the need to move in the world. Heavy things fly in space, she thinks, and sees herself lifting. Her thighs are still wet, clinging with mingled sweat. There's no space in the car to dress. She'll have to dress outside. He's been talking for minutes and is now waiting for her to say I love you. The night is darker over the quarry. She thinks of taking her clothes and dressing at the edge of that deeper dark, knowing the heaviness inside won't hold her to the earth.

46

Rising

We all stir, but we do not climb from our beds as she comes up the steps. I, awake in the room to the left at the top of the stairs, think of her as a fresh flower, sprouted from seeds beneath earth's surface, one now healthy and colorful and full of energy. Her buds will soon fill the stairwell. I will know not to rise and open my door when her limbs brush by. It shall be a light caress, I know, one I might have missed—though I understand now that I have no chance of not noticing.

47

A Country Walk With No Ambition

There is no new sun set free for it. It is always the same sun that chases the moon from the sky. Waving limbs make shadows dance along the rim of the browning field. Looking left to right, he's sure what he sees is new, just as it had been new yesterday. He believes his eyes, and gives no thought to what he might know. The woods grow darker. When swift monkeys clamber in a rush to be first to the throne, he joins their chant, grateful there is no one there to proselytize, only the flaming blast of leaves.

48

Bluebird Sky

It is perfectly natural for us to wish, each spring, that the bluebird has earned its color from its passage across blue sky, though we know this is not true. The bluebird is dependent on the sky for so much, but not for the color of its wings. We are all dependent on the sky for so much, and on the sea, although it's the bitterness of the end that sustains us. Bluebirds do not make gods of the changing expanse, or their constant movement, or the trees they light on for protection when sudden storms cleave a summer afternoon.

49

Like A Math Problem Looking For Its Car

It's not easy to be restless, standing atop this rock on the crashing coastline—or so some wise people will say, gesticulating serenity away with a movement of their hands or the tilt of an eyebrow. What if I am a pretend human? This is the question the voice inside longs to ask, and it is the question that should never be asked because it can never be answered. When I ponder it, and I ponder until I can feel my fingernails grow, I always end up thinking of how much I love the moon when it's only partly there.

50

Window

He has no melancholy, no remorse or unexplained sadness. He's sure of this—as he stands by the wide window with its surprising arrangement of small panes placed in a chaotic order that he spends hours trying to find some pattern of fragmented distress in, always coming up empty. All he touches or sees is empty, a vacuum he avoids the way his dreams will avoid places crowded with humans wandering around in parks looking for pleasure, or taking long walks with a determination that blinds them as they walk faster and faster, searching eagerly for remote sources of joy.

51

History

We were hunters once, when worthwhile things still came on the tip of a spear. After a kill, be it game or peace or tomorrow, we all felt the satisfaction only a hunter can feel. But after we first see History, there is no pageantry, only a boy with few clothes, working and sometimes sleeping, or romping across plowed fields—and not once does he turn to us, before slipping behind the fig bushes and blackberry vines at twilight to arc questions past the mule and the silver plow and over the rocks that gather skins and fall to powder.

52

Night Swimming

I once lived where night was the ocean of the world,
where if I wandered the pasture in the glow between
sundown and dark, toads came out and began their
dance. The crickets made a stereo of sound, and
excitement sat on my head like a crown. Have you
ever spent time in an old pasture, where mixtures of
light fill your insides like lava? You are a swimmer
in the bluing light, through the fence, past the barn
where the mules and ponies need no feed, where all
you think is, this may be my last moment on earth.

53

What Is Left Alongside Her

After I try again to separate the wind from the vane,
she cannot bear to talk of what remains. My words
tangle her in a truss of silence. But I stay, and climb
the stairs to stand outside her door. It's silly, on
the face of it, why I don't go in. That old, relentless
clock's consistency scorns all compassion as I wait
and think of my senseless victory. It is the clock's
tone that becomes a requiem of contempt for my
stubbornness. Its authority reminds me that I'm as
futile as the map that ends where the road forks.

54

All Fog is Gray

As he moves deeper into the room, toward the barred window, the door he'd passed through begins to slip away. The room is in a house in a town beside mountains with ragged peaks. When he reaches the window, the door has vanished. If he ever considers leaving, he must first remember the door is gone and accept that he must seek it out. The acceptance of necessity is the most difficult part of a task. Satisfied to find the window, he takes a breath. The fog begins to thicken and the peaks begin to fade. The fog is gray.

55

The End of Some THING

We all know nothing holds still, and each thing—.
Thing, a word that can be mated with another to
mean anything or everything or nothing, an ines-
capable word, a word that darts from the tongue's
tip faster than an ocean can fling a jellyfish to shore
when a storm settles over the horizon, or lift the sea
gulls dead on the deserted beach and drive them
out to the deep, out to where the inbound waves
crash, crash and roll from white to black, rolling in
the face of the outbound waves, like closing shut-
ters extinguishing a final light.

56

First Look Back

I have become a model prisoner. We spend nights in a cell, sleeping beneath a yellow light—and all of us, traveling across the small dirt yard presented to us on our first day, have progressed from wriggling on our stomachs, hands clasped to the small of our backs, to crawling at impressive speeds. The guards sit in chairs and seem committed to paying us no attention. On afternoons, we have classes devoted to the History of Ideas, with a focus on how their furtherance is our sole purpose. My excellence assures me I will be the first to walk.

57

Ghosting

Long before the professor dies, he's already sourced his ghost—but after his sight leaves him, and his hands can no longer reach his forehead, he realizes that he no longer remembers which ghost he's chosen. His specialty is Icelandic folk tales, but his ghost seems suited only for hot climates. He might remember—if only his mind could stop wandering back to his family, which had always been diligent and encouraged him, even as a boy, to begin searching out phantoms. "You may need one when you least expect it," they'd instructed. "It's wise to have an early start."

58

The Road Ahead

He knows the dust is not his face. He'd washed his face at that truck stop a few miles back and it had held together. Now he's in a race to make it to a place. The day is sunny and beautiful. The soft light melts across the road ahead. The truckers all seem happy, with an extra bounce to their step. They know without having to think that the world is everything—if only you can touch it. His tongue is thick. His eyes are dry, heavy under the dust. Everything is as it is intended to be. Yes.

59

One Night

We are happy all that night, sitting in our familiar circle while the dark decomposes around us. No one has fallen before sitting on their wicker chair, and at the end of the night, when our circle contracts and expands and then breaks into pieces like the last image lingering before death, everyone is still upright. The lights are out and around the porch a soft, fat evening wind buoys our arms as we reach out to touch one another and offer each our goodbyes. We are full that night, but unable to offer anything to those who are empty.

60

Night Bells

The chimes of the bells have ended and the night has thickened, and all around the limbs of the magnolia are bouncing. The wind continues to pick up until the world stands still and braces against its assault. But the world is wrong. The world is so often wrong. We have made our own circle, me and the trees and their dancing leaves. All the trees are smiling, and down the street windows are rising and new faces fill the expanse and we all sing the same song and even the bells lift their weary tongues and clap new chimes.

61

Moon Flag

The last I heard, the first flag on the moon is still standing. I'm choosing, today, to think about it. It's a memory, this flag on the moon, and memories don't come in precise order. First, I consider a bird, say a cardinal, thriving in its red industrialism—hunting, building, focused. This is where the cardinal and I differ. I seek sloth and can't find it. He is glorious in his plumage. I sit alone in a chair, which brings me back to the moon flag. Some say it's a miracle for me, and you, to be alive on earth.

62

Age Old Stones

Today my thoughts are all of coming apart. It's true the mind is a scythe few can wield without slaughter. Before I wake each morning from a stranger's sleep, there's a town in my dream marked by a shallow river where strong men once worked the forges. Rivers repeat their stories each season, and last night I stood in the dark band outside their circles of fire and pictured how, on a summer's day, weak winter's thin ice shines on the river stones—never wondering just how many summers the water must lick the stones before they turn to powder.

63

Creation Story

I make this mountain, this sea, the same way clouds linger as though they're born to water the stones and make sure the sea has ample moisture to keep the world alive. The mountain is a jagged peak too close to the changing tides. I should fix that, but it's a stubborn mountain, watching as the sea changes. It doesn't begrudge the water and is confident it will stand until erosion takes it down, while the sea is an endless enterprise, all of life below its surface, and it must maintain equilibrium, continually sending waves to collapse on the beach.

64

Outside The Gate

If you are alive, the past is buoyant and soft and bil-
lows a final sail full of charm; but we dead, we who
have only the past as present, we are immune to the
attraction of soft breezes and pregnant sails. No new
time raises its head to say, "I'm the current and this
day shall course through you like fire." There is no
new time. Stones fly, fire excites each hour, but the
suffering can never be surrendered to, so we walk
the ridge, suspended without support across the
bay that lures passing ships to dock at their doom.

65

End

My goal is to make another me—one carrying a sa-
ber, mysterious in my cunning. And from there it's
into the farther wilds, beyond that region, or the
other, which always fails to happen. Now, here I am,
a frog, or a penguin, any animal you prefer, it's of
no significance, and all I have to present is an end.
We, and I, who've no power to claim the beginning
of any blooming, and have no knowledge of the arc,
are claiming knowledge of the end—that I am here,
and you are there, and it is beyond our sight.

66

Lies

If you do that often enough you will go in circles. Circles with no integrity, weaving, starting and stopping. Only from a distance impossible to attain does the stumbling resemble a circle, though even in the middle of making one you know it's not a line. It's a hustle, this idea of moving in a line. A myth of going places. A mirror at impossible angles. I have too much to tell you to start off with a lie. The lies will come later. No curtains will be opened in the end, no falsehood will be father of the truth.

67

Light

The sun is blasting my scrabbled expanse and I cannot breathe. I traveled here with no star, no map, no direction, only the guidance of the first words and the determined straightness of my feet. The dark is behind me now, I am cast into this light that cuts through my skin. I will never be able to continue this way. My feet are cracked and my hands bleed. Now—a vigil in this exterminating light, where everything is known, everything is seen, everything can be experienced, until the light, the knowing light, bores through the final thread of darkness.

68

Hands

Standing on the hill each evening, after a day of possessing and dispossessing, there is nothing left to be done but, first, to wave your arms toward the full distance, and then to stare toward the bottom of the hill, the feet of the old hill, which seems surrounded now by the wave of what may be hands billowing up and down at a steady pace. It's impossible to feel certainty, standing on top of this hill, unmovable the way yesterday is unmovable, craning a neck, bending forward to feel the soft lift of wind arising from the waving hands.

69

Lambs

He's a hundred years old on the day he's born, and lives a second hundred years with his lambs in a pasture—though he prefers those few who stop eating and walk slowly to the dry or muddy barnyard, soundlessly gazing back toward the remainder of the small flock still grazing in the fenced pasture. Such gazes promise nothing for lambs who learn nothing on their long journey through the firelight tunnel, from the slopes of Mount Olive to the Mount of Corruption—to this place, where, if you close your eyes, you see only lambs staring across the barnyard.

70

Green

If you don't insist on knowing, you can imagine being where knotty green love grows so fast in summer you have to pick it every day, where women work all night stroking and cleaning and preparing love for pickling—rows of women in consistent motion. Consider that symmetry! If you can see that picture forever in the eye between your eyes, in the eye in the center of your forehead which you may not have been blessed with, the eye that sees—perhaps even someone as dull as you will understand how some know the green that has never left.

71

Street

I'm scheduled to explain the odors of flowers—yet I hide in a house to avoid the listeners. They are gathering outside, along the street. Mothers, daughters, several sons, two or three fathers, some horses, wagons, one hauling a Gatling gun. They're all hungry. There's a dog, needed to scout provisions. Another dog squats at the base of the oak, squirrels flitting overhead. I watch them through my window, milling about, lost and lonely and so blind in their small circle—the old man, their leader, leaning seven, maybe nine degrees to the right, hand resting on his son's shoulder.

72

Fingertips

He doesn't like his fingertips to brush up against the thinning patch of his uncombed hair, but they are given no other option—because the urge of the bulge of his forehead, its soft firm ridge slightly protruding from beneath the hairline, has to settle neatly into the cup of his palms. It's a comfortable fit, without need of finger adjustment. Although, if his sleeves are the tiniest bit too short, his eyebrows, which are aggressively bushy, tickle his wrists and slightly diminish the consolation that quiet brings, living here alone in the white-framed house which his aunt willed him.

73

Blinking

After his resurrection, the children begin to play. They run through the house with brooms between their legs. "I'm a bigger witch!" "I'm older and uglier and meaner!" On the street below his window, men and women wait with cameras and phones. He has a clipboard with a list of unanswered questions. The crowd continues swelling and the flashbulbs are ceaseless. At dusk the children on the street take out silver balloons that seem to multiply as they spread among the crowd. An agreement is reached—not to release the balloons until morning. Near midnight the cameras finally stop blinking.

74

Food

He's been dead a thousand years, but is always a vis-
itor. He travels from town to town to town. The peo-
ple in each town welcome him. Make a home here,
they say. Stop wandering. This is an empty world. A
vast expanse of bliss leaves him untouched. Nights,
he builds a fire and thinks about the taste of roast-
ed beef and the thick threads at the heart of sweet
potatoes. Crispy bacon with tomatoes and toast. As
the years go by, his remembered life grows larger
and he begins to stand taller and is not always alone
in his travels.

75

Blue Petals

She tends her garden in a nun's habit bought in a second-hand shop, trims the shrubs, mows the grass with a push-mower, dreams of a garden like the one the nuns nourish—blue flowers blooming in fragile petals, thin roots slipping through the soil in need of watering daily, such slight plants, lovelier than the green sturdy shrubs she trims with a set of cutters so heavy her shoulders ache and her wrists ring with pain echoing up her arms as she dresses for bed in the cotton gown that sweeps across her feet when she kneels beside her bunk.

76

Away

He is not a slave of the sword. No violence, no nailed words spit across campfires, tatter his cape. The dark is not full, he learned as a child, and he has spent no time trying to fill it. He spends no time filling anything or anyone and protects his well of emptiness as though it were gold. He sits alone in his room in the attic of the old house. One window looks out over a sea of waving trees. There is nothing in the trees to see except the way they lean away when the wind rushes forward.

77

Shearing

Is it time to shear the lambs? To caress their full coats, to watch the knots of wool part beneath your fingers? It's a wet spring, the ground sucks at your feet as you walk out across the muddy field. The lambs, living in the pasture beyond the barn, wait patiently for you to come with your shears, wait to have the weight of their winter existence removed so you and they can gather your resources, your contentment, to face the coming rage of heat. You'll join them in their struggle, wandering through trees on the far sides of fences.

78

Apartments

The woman who lives on the first floor once loved dancing naked for her lovers. Now she is acquainted with winter days that never turn from gray. The girl who lives in the apartment above never sings when her lover visits. But when she is alone, she sings with a voice that clings to its lightness. When the lover leaves, he hurries downstairs, and the door of the old apartment building bangs shut. Then the woman on the first floor stops all her chores and sits at her dining table with two chairs and waits for the girl to sing.

79

Stay

You can stay where you are, unconcerned about what may or may not be waiting outside the closed door. The window's closed too, and there will never be reason to rise from your seat at the empty desk and walk to the glass to discover what may be, or bend over and lay your gaze across the desk's polished surface. Ask yourself—is this where it should rest? Soon you'll discover there's no need of expanses to discover nothing, it dwells on every surface, even there beneath the open books, fallen face down, strewn across the floor beyond your chair.

80

Selfish

The young girl who lives in the white room cannot remember when she last loved her lover. She remembers the nights they made love, how afterward he'd fall asleep, and how she'd watch him sleep, smiling at the way his girlish lips made a pout as his breaths blew in and out. She knew he was dreaming and wouldn't remember the dream the next day. Now the love has left, and though she can remember those nights, she cannot remember loving him. While he sleeps, she reads all through the night— and thinks, there is nothing so selfish as sleep.

81

Silver

All is like silver—willowy, never-dull silver—he is
alive only at night wandering the circle of his re-
straint, seeking shelter in the farthest extents of
what he can only dream of—for he can never imag-
ine such a distance, such a relaxation of the madness
of coming, of the contentment of being, of opening
his arms to leaving. There may be a reckoning, but
not the dead reckoning of a sailor contained by his
sea—rather the reckoning sung each morning by
crows and the smaller, more colorful birds that fly
from tree to tree in the near distance.

82

Marsh

She longs to live marsh-side, where the fragrance of rich water and seldom traveled sea is so heavy it will soon become a permanent memory. She longs—although she feels there is fright there, as she moves even closer, her now heavy legs grown weary, her womb expanded, her breasts full of milk—and she lies down beside the moving reeds and smiles at the sky busy with moving clouds, and she sings the birth, slips into and out of dreams until the crying begins. She softly rises to her feet and walks beyond—the crying, the safe crying, behind.

83

Temples

I take the crack of my old bones, the ceased flowing of lost ambitions, wrap them around the final field to build a temple in which I will store masks, rotten cloaks, the last rusted armor. From the front, I set the fire which frees me for a walk across the lake that masks the silver bed where fish have swept the years along with forward faces and sideways glances. I am older now than all the gods—and newer than the screams of all the sheep, the blood that flows through every temple, the song of sirens singing home.

84

Magician

He thinks of himself as a magician and allows this belief to make him content. He walks across town, or into the forests and swamps that surround it, with hands behind his back, head bent forward. The soil beneath his feet promises a spring, an extra step if needed, and so he becomes aware of the need to hurry—for hurry is something magicians must master. How else can he hope to be available when the call for help emerged from the less gifted sounds? How else can he hope to light the minds of those who see him walking?

85

Rocks

No rocks to shatter on!—the captain screams across
the flooded extremes, all sound, all voice flying over
the buttonbush and sedge of the marsh, diving into
dark, deep water. The captain thinks of a shatter-
ing that might occur if he could pray for it—how it
would splinter all he could see until there was no
more to see, only a rage burning a roaring sea, noth-
ing left to shatter. Now, what shall a man see and
say at the very end of such an end? So many voices
imagined, each one unattainable by the voice of the
captain.

86

Quiet

So much of his time is spent in the unfettered quiet, in that obsessive quiet that forces each soft sound or the echo of each voice, into banishment, into the container of ending—that's what he has come to call it—now that he already knows all that wells up inside him, from the almost unintelligible sound of drops dripping, dripping, to the more lilting sound of the song he composes there, in his quiet enclave, the song he can never hear as he watches it walk the empty terrain, allowing him to maintain his position, unflinching in his role.

87

Dwellers

Beneath the building, there are many things to say, although no one knows how to talk. The tiny dwellers spend their days wondering why no words come from their mouths. It's their only puzzle, and for generations, the wisest have been anointed with dust, and with the water that seeps from the thick pipes. After anointment, the wisest dweller gathers his compatriots to begin again, first mouthing hopeful shouts, and then gesticulating, always to no avail. There was once, generations before, much conflict about their failure to speak and the tribe suffered. When weariness arrives, they sleep in a circle.

88

Walls

Each time he turns to face the wall he knows there's
no more to study. Seeing himself as a creature of
the mind?—that's all gone. He's grateful for the
awareness the wall provides, but is incapable, de-
spite his determination, to remain in that position,
spine straight, hands unclasped, waiting for a gen-
tleness softer than the small breeze that sometimes
comes as he asks himself again why he cannot con-
tinue tracing the cracks in the dried mud that holds
the stones in place—while the sun sets and crows
light on the wall's top to study the broad country-
side beyond.

89

Mirage

It isn't until the last mirage collapses. And that isn't merely because she's at last moved closer. It's when she stands, silent, like one of the huge stones crowding round her, never approaching the series of mirages rippling far as her gaze, that she catches sight of the man, collapsed like a gone ghost, lying face-down, almost covered by the fabric of weeds encircling him. When she does move closer, walking lightly to his side and softly bending down, she sees that he is alive, his eyes intently staring into the soil, a smile of utmost contentment on his face.

90

Heaven

Heaven is a border that exists because one god, an eternity ago, decided that all things needed borders. How else can infinity be realized without borders to point across and say, "That is not infinity." This god's wisdom (and no one now knows which god it was) thus spoke: Borders! Yet how can the infinite be boundaried? The angels are trapped now in a paradise that's no longer a paradise because its wall presses against them, regardless of how distant it is. The border is everywhere, the residents know, and this narrows the joy of those who are not gods.

91

Clandestine

On these long days, I walk with a limp and carry many clandestine things—worlds of three dead dogs, words of muddy dead men, smiles of devoted beasts. More than can be remembered waits to be unloaded. I'm convinced there's a brow strong enough to bear the pressure that bears me over the arc to where bells ripen, bending softly, their sounds too soft to echo a second and third whisper. Allow me to put down these lines here—here where the last mercury has one more chance—here with the lonely ax, the rusted knee, the last angle, sleep.

92

I Knew Her

We met in the theater. I did the lighting. She ran lines in bed. During the day we drank. She's coming back to me. She said I was a fake. Her shoulder blades angled like swords that will never cross. I think this is right. One night she told me to leave. My hands were full. She opened the door. We knew we would end but I never knew she would get lost in the mind of a man who best recalls her saying, "You fucked the life out of me," one night, in the dark, before we fell asleep.

93

Grief Thievery

I press against the marble wall of the Mourning Hall. I wish I could stand quietly, but I cannot stop moving—like a hungry man outside a restaurant window. It's all for nothing. The grief there is not mine, and the world is a selfish place. A silver-haired widow stands in the middle of the floor, stored tears gathering in the corners of her eyes. Crying does not come easy. Tears wasted in her youth before grief was rationed are now a source of regret. Inured to the longing of the griefless, she'll protect her tears, her agony, like contraband.

94

Worms And Horses

In his first city, bodies were buried in small grave-
yards behind small churches. That city was old, as
old as cities can be where horses once failed to ex-
ist. Cold, in this city, but not as blindingly cold—
he walks nights, sees a white horse pristine against
sooty snow. Perhaps he sees the horse only because
he already knows the worms of those other cities of
the dead he once arrived in—empty-handed, think-
ing only of what's underground, never understand-
ing the white horse that's wearied of a history that
doesn't free him. I'm here, he whispers. No one is
listening.

95

Note

In the bright light of a late afternoon, the villagers come out from their homes, and the forest dwellers emerge from vine-bordered woods that haunt the villagers with vast expanses and endless darknesses they cannot understand. They're waiting now, all of them, for the arrival of the letter they all long for. They've agreed—on this day one will not kill the other, nor take their family as slaves, while they await the note said to be so full of suffering that all their own suffering will end once they rip open the envelope and sing out the words inside.

96

Nothing

Today I search for Nothing and discover Nothing is a tree, appealing in its strength, in the gold tints of the bark, in the sharp tips of the thick, widening leaves. Nothing tempts one to stand before it, to think only of its long, sturdy roots threading through the red soil—for the earth is always red where I stand. But now my cough has returned and Nothing becomes the heaving of my chest, the force faltering from my lungs until Nothing gives way to dark air and becomes visible, like wide wings floating closer and closer to a cliff.

97

Banishment

Why must I die each time I cross the dry plain and climb the slope, there to place on the precipice the dregs of my discontent and loss? These are not the thoughts an eagle has, nor does the eagle fret about banishment each time he finds a place to make his home—he'll mate, perhaps in a fury of feathers, then will release his grip, returning to the ledge that's now his heaven, to watch the thickening night, alert to any danger, alive in his stillness, with no need of a halo of grace on his ledge of contentment.

98

Contours

Oceans have no sides, only contours—which may
mean (I almost wrote must mean) all things once
moved by magic now have a need to exist not creat-
ed by the container in which they rest. The smallest
poplar grows away from its roots the deeper those
roots dig into the soil. Tonight, when twilight be-
gins to fill the thicket of trees and vines, and the
field grass softens into brown as it glides up from
the brackish creek, a covey of quail blusters into a
cloud of white, brown, and black, all with traces of
blue on their leonine necks.

99

The Glow

Here is a garden with a short wall made of white stones. Inside, the rows lie measured apart, each planted with crops we never touch. There is a brook and a there is a tree—and beyond, a relentless glow. The small girl lives in the cage hanging from the tree. She's grown, and so the thinner, upper limb is beginning to bend. She must be lowered to a sturdier limb. First, there'll be discussion. Who'll perform the task? Who'll help? And how much information will be shared with the child? It is a task we each want to avoid.

100

Free Labor

He labors every day with hoe and spade, hour by hour, even when no task is there to curtsy before him like the last girl he knew before he came here, before he walked the rock-strewn miles, bent forward at the waist, weary head pressed against the endless magic of the wind. The tomatoes have rotted on their vines, the peas are dried and dead, the potatoes full of blind-black eyes in the ground—he hoes and chops, head full of the glory of ground cracking beneath his blows, rocks avoided, bees swirling as the day drifts toward its end.

About The Author

John Riley was born in Los Angeles, but grew up in John Coltrane's hometown. He worked for many years in an educational publishing company he founded with his wife. He has published fiction, poetry, and nonfiction in many journals and has written over forty books of nonfiction. He lives in Greensboro, North Carolina.

Other Titles Available From Exot Books

Black Uncle, John Marcus Powell ~ 2023
Pools of June, Mary Meriam ~ 2022
Huncke, Rick Mullin ~ 2021
Schnauzer, David Yezzi ~ 2018
Veil On, Veil Off, John Marcus Powell ~ 2018
A Special Education, Meredith Bergmann ~ 2014
Glorious Babe, John Marcus Powell ~ 2014
Questions, Richard Loranger/Bill Mercer ~ 2013
Turn, Ann Drysdale ~ 2013
Tomorrow & Tomorrow, David Yezzi ~ 2013
Facing The Remains, Tom Merrill ~ 2012
Blue Wins Forever, Paco Brown ~ 2012
They Can Keep The Cinderblock, Mike Lane ~ 2012
Colors, Jay Chollick ~ 2011
Loony Lovers, John Marcus Powell ~ 2011
Filled With Breath: 30 Sonnets by 30 Poets, ed. Mary Meriam ~ 2010
Let Me Be Like Glass, Adriana Scopino ~ 2010
What's That Supposed To Mean, Wendy Videlock ~ 2010
We Internet In Different Voices, Mike Alexander ~ 2009
11 Films, Jane Ormerod ~ 2008
Aquinas Flinched, Rick Mullin ~ 2008
Graceways, Austin MacRae ~ 2008
Prospero At Breakfast, Alan Wickes ~ 2008
Sometime Before The Bell, Ray Pospisil ~ 2006
The Countess Of Flatbroke, Mary Meriam ~ 2006
Blue Glass Cities, Mark Allinson ~ 2006
Prolegomena To An Essay On Satire, R. Nemo Hill ~2006
William Montgomery, Quincy R. Lehr ~ 2006

ORDER ONLINE AT exotbooks.com

Ingram Content Group UK Ltd.
Milton Keynes UK
UKHW010636200723
425492UK00004B/299

9 780989 898478